Kansas
on my mind

FALCON PRESS

The Wichita Eagle

Kansas prairie vision: butterfly milkweed blooming on the Konza Prairie near Manhattan   FRANK OBERLE

introduction

I was nineteen years old when I left Kansas in the early 60s to join the Air Force and see the world. And like most young Kansans I had done a miserable job of getting to know my native state.

Up until that time my knowledge of our state was what went on in Newton mixed in with my daily trips into Wichita where I labored as a grain sampler for the Kansas State Grain Inspection Department.

During the better part of the next decade I spent portions of my life in Texas, Nebraska, Guam, back to Kansas for a short time, then three years scratching out an undergraduate degree in Santa Barbara, California.

The seed of exploration germinated during those years. First in Nebraska with weekend trips to explore small farm communities, later on Guam where I moved from the barracks to live and become part of village life in Mangilao. And finally in California where I realized that the only way you can get to know a place is to hit the road and explore it.

And so it was that in October 1971, two days after my graduation, I packed up my Volkswagen bus, bid goodbye to my beloved Santa Barbara, and hit the road for Kansas. I felt drawn by some latent prairie roots which had a firm grip on my soul, pulling me back to teach me, in three dimensional terms, what it means to be a Kansan.

That first year back at the home place was filled with sensory overload as I absorbed the full spectrum of the four seasons I had missed while living on the coast.

Fall colors, something I had been deprived of for three years, dazzled my senses and reawakened my forgotten love of a chilly fall day. Shimmering yellow cottonwood leaves danced against an electric blue sky laced with puffy white clouds. And below, rust-red grasses of the Sand Hills prairie swayed on a cool breeze.

At Halloween, groups of children, decked out in homemade and store-bought costumes, went from door-to-door to glean a trick-or-treat bounty from their friends and neighbors.

Hand-carved pumpkins, their faces lighted with the yellow glow of flickering candles, glared from on porch posts and steps, each reflecting a homemade greeting to hordes of miniature goblins.

On Friday night the arched glow of stadium lights illuminated the black, star-dotted sky over Athletic Park while the sounds of cheering football fans filled the air as they huddled, wrapped in blankets, to ward off the chill of a crisp fall night.

Christmas in Harvey County took on a homey feeling as each of the surrounding towns, large and small, did its best to decorate and get into the spirit of the season. And all across the state churches and schools filled each night with school children and parishioners who celebrated the season with programs and song.

And then there was the crystal clarity of a hard winter, that two-edged season which caps off the fall and spawns the spring. The snow came early to Kansas that year and with it an elegant weave of red and orange leaves stitched together with an icy white lace.

The first snowfall of that memorable winter drew me outside like a bug to a light, standing there like a fool, transfixed by the crystalline flakes falling gently from the cold, black night.

And all through the winter, no matter how harsh it became, I was constantly reminded of spring's promise by the green carpet of hard red winter wheat which covered most of central Kansas.

Then came spring with its driving rains and brooding skies topped with massive thunderheads. Electrical storms crackled through the night, remin-

Mount Sunflower, the highest point in Kansas, Wallace County
MIKE BLAIR

4

ding me of why Kansans have basements and Californians don't.

But with the storms also came an incredible mosaic of flowering plants reflecting every color imaginable, particularly the wildflowers which bloomed in a helter-skelter fashion across the lush Flint Hills prairie.

Behind the spring storms lay the long, hot summer. In late May the wheat, which had been green through winter and spring, began to change color at the base of each shaft. Green turned to gold as the days grew hotter and drier. And by early June the wind-driven waves of amber grain were ready for harvest.

All through June and July massive combines lumbered across Kansas, following the ripening wheat from south to north. Every county road and small town grain elevator bustled with the task of bringing in, transporting, and storing another harvest of prairie gold.

Thousands of Kansans—men and women, boys and girls—toiled day and night, all the while building memories based on the hot, gritty task of bringing in another year's bounty.

It was during that first summer back home that I decided to explore beyond what I already knew. In those first ten months I had re-experienced many things I had taken for granted, and I found those sensory experiences to be at the heart of why I wanted to live in Kansas.

But from my travels I knew that what I had experienced around Harvey County represented only a minute amount of what could be found in the other 104 counties. And so in 1972 I began an odyssey which has taken me to every county in Kansas, most of them several times.

My first eye opener of a trip was to the Flint Hills of Chase County, only forty miles east of Newton. It's funny how you can grow up in a place and never know what is around you, but when I made that turn north at Cassoday my life changed forever.

For the first time I saw lush, green, rolling hills dotted with cattle. In the valleys between the hills ran clear, spring-fed streams lined with cottonwood, sycamore, and oak trees. And in the streams were abundant native populations of channel catfish, spotted bass, and other species of sunfish.

The highway from Cassoday to Cottonwood Falls wasn't straight like I was accustomed to in the Arkansas River Lowlands where I had grown up. Instead it was hilly and winding as it threaded its way through the Valley of the South Fork.

Every so often there would be a side road which beckoned me to sample what it had to offer. It was like a cornucopia of opportunities, too much for a small-town boy who grew up accustomed to land divided into square miles. I was used to always having a grain elevator in sight to keep my bearings. The thought of becoming lost in Kansas

Towering thunderheads fill a spring sky in Reno County STEVE HARPER

was more than a little intriguing.

The most delightful part of that first Kansas sojourn was when I took one of those side roads that ended up at a low-water crossing over the South Fork. I stopped my bus halfway across the river, opened the side door, sat on the edge of the floor, and dangled my feet in the cool rushing waters.

I knew then that I had missed a great deal of what Kansas had to offer during my first twenty-seven years, and that I would dedicate the rest of my life to the exploration of my native state.

Since that first outing I have come to know the four corners of Kansas which are as different as four snowflakes.

Perhaps the least known area is the Arikaree Breaks of Cheyenne County where arid canyons break up the rolling hills surrounding the Arikaree River, as the river makes a short passage through Kansas on its way from Colorado to Nebraska.

The Republican River enters Kansas as a narrow, High-Plains stream bordered by thick woodlands alive with wild turkeys, mule deer, and bobcat. A tough, semi-arid land inhabited by tough but friendly people who put on one of Kansas' finest county fairs each August in St. Francis.

In the northeast corner are the rolling loess hills of Doniphan County. At White Cloud I stood on a towering hill overlooking the Missouri River. From that lofty vantage point it was easy to imagine what the area looked like when thirty to forty riverboats docked there each day in the days following the Civil War.

Cherokee County in the southeast corner offers the tangled, rugged beauty of the Ozark Plateau. Its landscape, once ravaged by the mining of coal, lead, and zinc has slowly healed and is rapidly becoming a tourist destination.

In the southwest corner is the 108,000 acres of Cimarron National Grasslands of Morton County. It is the largest area of public land in Kansas and offers an inviting blend of outdoor experiences for hikers, campers, hunters, and history buffs.

On my first trip to Morton County I watched lesser prairie chickens at dawn on their ancient booming grounds. In the evening I visited Point of Rocks, a natural landmark for travelers heading southwest on the Santa Fe Trail. As the sun neared the horizon I watched as three mule deer bedded down along the wooded banks of the Cimarron River.

As the red glow of day faded to the blue of twilight, a pack of coyotes struck up a multiple-part

harmony on the sand-sage prairie to the north. Their howls and yips where quickly answered by a roosting gobbler who scolded them for disturbing his sleep.

After visiting the four corners I got an opportunity to see Kansas from the river when I spent two-and-a-half days on a small boat traveling upstream on the Missouri from Kansas City to White Cloud.

Experiencing Kansas at frontier river ports like Leavenworth, Atchison, Elwood, and White Cloud gave me a new perspective on the winding gash of a corner which keeps Kansas from being a perfect rectangle.

I also found wonder and beauty in other parts of Kansas.

The Gypsum Hills of Barber, Comanche, Kiowa, and Clark Counties surprised me like no other area in Kansas. Red, flat-topped hills dotted with cedars are not figments of the old west, but rather what continues to be a place steeped in western traditions and lifestyles.

The rugged hills, teeming with wildlife, offer a breathtaking panorama. It's a place where sprawling, unfenced rangeland is common, and the people are as friendly and open as the place they live.

Coronado Heights in the Smoky Hills of north-central Kansas is a fine, high vantage point to watch a sunrise over the verdant valley to the east. It was

Start of the annual Bank IV River Run, Wichita LARRY FLEMING

in that area where Coronado and his soldiers passed to the north in the 1500s as they searched in vain for the Seven Cities of Gold.

In the southeast part of Kansas are the rolling, escarpment-lined plains which evolve from prairie into tree-covered woodlands whose valleys are lined with rivers like the Neosho, Verdigris, Caney, and the Marais des Cygnes.

Even in all my travels across Kansas since 1972, I realize now that I have only scratched the surface of what our state has to offer. Kansas has an abundance of natural resources, fascinating historical significance, and varied landscapes topped with mind-blowing sunrises and sunsets.

Add to those things the strength of character and friendliness of the folks who live in small towns like Cedar Vale, Troy, Atwood, Valley Falls, and Sun City, and you have found the heart and soul of what makes Kansas one of the finest places in the world to live and raise a family.

Because in the end it is the people of a state that make it great. And Kansans, the "People of the South Wind," are the finest people I have ever met.

Steve Harper,
Newton

Training a harness horse in Coffeyville   MIKE LOGAN

7

Wheat harvest near Lenora, Norton County   DANIEL DANCER

Princess Plume at Castle City in Gove County   DANIEL DANCER

Prairie wildflowers in the Flint Hills   FRANK OBERLE

" *If I had to choose between Heaven and Kansas, I'd choose Kansas.* "

Jane Koger
Chase County rancher

Weeping willow on a shallow pond in Cherokee County   DANIEL DANCER

A family of raccoons at the Chaplin Nature Center, Arkansas City   GERALD J. WIENS

A flowering catalpa tree on the shore of West Lake in Harvey County   STEVE HARPER

Long-leaved phlox blooming brightly in Shawnee County   STEVE MULLIGAN

A cloudless sulphur butterfly visiting a musk thistle in Cowley County   STEVE HARPER

Fox Creek Schoolhouse and purple coneflowers on the Z-Bar Ranch in the Flint Hills, near Strong City   FRANK OBERLE

14

Yucca plants in full bloom near the Smoky Hill River in western Kansas   TOM TILL

Enjoying Indian blanket wildflowers on the prairie near Pratt in Pratt County   MIKE BLAIR

Whitetail fawn resting amid milkweed, Reno County   MIKE BLAIR

Thick thunderheads in Chase County   DANIEL DANCER

" *Kansans are a race of sky-watchers. Of course the sky is everywhere around us in this land of far horizons: it constantly impinges upon the Kansas consciousness. Even where the land is heaped and rolled over lime or sandstone undergirdings, three fourths or more of any person's level view across it in any direction consists of heavenly space and light with whatever cloud formations drift over it....* "

Kenneth S. Davis
"Portrait of a Changing Kansas"

Summer storm advancing on a farm in Harvey County   STEVE HARPER

A wheat harvester watching the sky in Greeley County   DANIEL DANCER

A golden field of wheat stretching to the horizon near Goodland   FRANK OBERLE

Harvesting wheat, Kansas' king of crops, near Winfield   JOEL SARTORE

Farmer waiting to unload grain in Elbing   JOEL SARTORE

A summer sunset firing the sky over St. Benedict's Church in St. Benedict, Nemaha County   DANIEL DANCER

" *Kansas is a zone beyond the peopled horizon and beyond all time where only the best part of the human spirit walks, touching both earth and sky at once.* "

Denise Low,
"Touching the Sky"

Cathedral of the Plains (St. Fidelis Church), built from native limestone and completed in 1911, in Victoria   STEVE HARPER

Simple but sturdy, a well-worn pew in the Church of Christ in Hewins, Chautauqua County   STEVE HARPER

Morning reflections of cattails and cottonwoods at Cheney State Park and Reservoir in Reno County STEVE MULLIGAN

Sandhill cranes displaying at Cheyenne Bottoms, a state wildlife area northeast of Great Bend   FRANK OBERLE

" *This country presents a fine appearance, the like of which I have not seen a better in all our Spain nor Italy, nor a part of France, nor . . . in the other countries where I have traveled in His Majesty's service, for it is not a very rough country, but is made up of hillocks and plains, and very fine-appearing rivers and streams, which certainly satisfied me and made me sure that it will be very fruitful in all sorts of products.* "

Comments on the Kansas area from the journal of Juan Jaramillo,
a horseman who in 1540 rode with Spanish explorer Francisco Vasquez de Coronado

Keeper of the Plains at the Mid-America All-Indian Center, Wichita   DANIEL DANCER

Traditional dancer at the Inter-Tribal Warrior Society Annual Pow-wow, Wichita   ANTHONY REED

Young dancer at the Kickapoo Pow-wow, Norton
NATHAN HAM

> " *I was born on the prairie,
> where the wind blew free and there
> was nothing to break the light of
> the sun . . . and where everything
> drew a free breath.* "

Parra-Wa-Samen (Ten Bears)
of the Yamparika Comanches,
Treaty speech of 1872

One of the 200 bison at the 2,200-acre Maxwell Wildlife Refuge near McPherson   DANIEL DANCER

Swift fox kits playing near Sharon Springs, Wallace County   MIKE BLAIR

Portrait of a bald eagle at the Chaplin Nature Center in Arkansas City   GERALD J. WIENS

Purple coneflowers blooming on the Konza Prairie, south of Manhattan   FRANK OBERLE

" *The prairie doesn't give up anything easily, unless it's horizon and sky.* **"**

William Least Heat-Moon,
PrairyErth

Prairie skirmish near Sawyer, Barber County   MIKE BLAIR

Point of Rocks in Cimarron National Grasslands, Morton County STEVE MULLIGAN

Commercial sunflowers bowing before an approaching thunderstorm in Marion County   STEVE HARPER

> **"** *They call Kansas the 'Sunflower State'. . .because, as the sunflower turns on its stem to catch the first beams of the morning sun, and with its broad disk and yellow rays follows the great orb of the day, so Kansas turns to catch the first rays of every advancing thought or civilized agency, and with her broad prairies and golden fields welcomes and follows the light.* **"**

Editorial in the Burlington Nonpareil (1887)

Turning towards the sun   LARRY FLEMING

Wichita's skyline above A. Price Woodard Park along the Arkansas River   STEVE HARPER

   " *So what is the truth of Kansas?. . . .It is the heartland of America, indeed, but not simply in the way popularly understood; it also beats at our center because, like the whole nation, it moves in turbulence, in fitfulness, and, somehow between times, in beauty.* **"**

William Least Heat-Moon,
"The Great Kansas Passage"

Cannons firing on cue as the Wichita Symphony plays the 1812 Overture during the annual Wichita River Festival   STEVE HARPER

Assembling a Citation II business jet at the
Cessna Aircraft Company in Wichita   JOEL SARTORE

Sedgwick County Courthouse, Wichita   BOB BARRETT

Having fun on the restored antique carousel at Gage Park, Topeka   BOB BARRETT

Father and son at Clark County State Fishing Lake near Kingsdown   STEVE HARPER

Railroad tracks disappearing into the distance near Plevna, Reno County   STEVE HARPER

Maintaining the old ways: an Amish carriage in Reno County   DANIEL DANCER

Electrifying sight in Chase County   DANIEL DANCER

Challenging the Kansas wind   GEORGE OLSON

" *[The stranger to Kansas],
if he listened to the voice of
experience, would not start upon
his pilgrimage at any season of
the year without an overcoat, a
fan, a lightning rod, and an
umbrella.* "

John James Ingalls,
''Blue Grass''

Big bluestem grass stretching to a far horizon at the Konza Prairie Natural Research Area, Riley County   STEVE MULLIGAN

“No mountains can be as beautiful for me as the far horizon, level as a floor, 20 or 30 miles in the distance. The sight fills me with a wonderful feeling of personal freedom, and also with a sense of infinity. Man finds his solitude here and . . .cannot help but wonder about the nature of all being.”

William Inge,
''A Level Land''

Sunset at Konza Prairie   STEVE MULLIGAN

Castle Rock, seventy-foot-high landmark for pioneers along the Butterfield Trail, Gove County   STEVE MULLIGAN

One of the namesake formations at Mushroom Rock State Park, east of Ellsworth   STEVE HARPER

66 *To understand why people say 'Dear old Kansas!'
is to understand that Kansas is no mere geographical
expression, but a 'state of mind,' a religion, and a
philosophy in one.* 99

Carl L. Becker,
''Kansas''

A beautiful Kansas morning in southern Harvey County   STEVE HARPER

"*These things—the air, the water, the scenery and we who fill these scenes—hold many and many a man to Kansas when money would tempt him away....Here are the still waters, here are the green pastures. Here, the fairest of the world's habitations.*"

William Allen White

Stan Herd's "Sunflowers in a Vase" field art near Eudora, Douglas County   LARRY FLEMING

Community mural in Marquette, McPherson County   GEORGE OLSON

Horses chasing the shadow of a hot-air balloon in Sedgwick County   STEVE HARPER

Heading home on Kanopolis Reservoir, Ellsworth County   STEVE HARPER

Harvesting wheat in Harvey County   STEVE HARPER

" *Across this open prairie,*
rolls Kansas far and wide,
    Surrounded now by wheat fields,
where cowboys used to ride . . . .
    And the air so clear on a given day,
you can see for many a mile.
    And coming home to Kansas
is like the warmth of your best
friend's smile. "

Phyllis Macy-Mills,
Cedar Vale songwriter,
quoted in Kansas People

Fall fun in Mound City, Linn County   MIKE BLAIR

Snowstorm in Gypsum, Saline County GEORGE OLSON

Cottontail rabbit sunning in eastern Kansas FRANK OBERLE

Sunflower stalks and snowdrifts at Logan State Park, Logan County   STEVE MULLIGAN

48

Sassafras and sumac in autumn splendor at Shermerhorn Park, Cherokee County   STEVE MULLIGAN

Bluejacket sandstone at Shermerhorn Park near Galena, Cherokee County   STEVE MULLIGAN

" *Kansas is a diverse state, in land form, waterway, weather, and wildlife. Four hundred and eleven miles wide and 207 miles between its northern and southern borders, it is not at all monotonous to those possessed of curiosity about their surroundings.* "

Joseph Collins,
Natural Kansas

Great-horned owl in a bur oak, Sedgwick County BOB GRESS

A whitetail buck venturing into a field in Lyon County   STEVE HARPER

Fall wildflowers in the Gypsum Hills, Barber County   DANIEL DANCER

Butterfly milkweed in the Chautauqua Hills STEVE HARPER

Prickly pear cactus, Ford County STEVE HARPER

Barrel cactus, Barber County MIKE BLAIR

Dawn at Cedar Bluffs State Park, fossil-rich scenic area along the Smoky Hill River, Trego County   STEVE MULLIGAN

" I can remember exactly how the country looked to me as I walked beside my grandmother along the faint wagontracks on that early November morning . . . for more than anything else I felt motion in the landscape: in the fresh, easy flowing morning wind . . . and in the earth itself . . . as if the shaggy grass were sort of loose hide . . . and underneath it herds of wild buffalo were galloping, galloping. "

Willa Cather,
My Antonia

Pioneer girl at the Hillsboro Arts and Crafts Fair   NATHAN HAM

Sunrise on the prairie at the Maxwell Wildlife Refuge, McPherson County   MIKE BLAIR

Goldenrod and blazing star wildflowers at Konza Prairie   FRANK OBERLE

Prairie bluebells in the Smoky Hills, Ellsworth County   STEVE HARPER

Prairie nest of a red-winged blackbird   FRANK OBERLE

Luna moth in eastern Kansas   BOB GRESS

Bringing the Wild West back to life at the Boot Hill Museum, Dodge City   JOHN AVERY / PHOTOGRAPHIC RESOURCES

The historic Lunt Home, a Queen Anne style house built in 1887, Fort Scott
JOHN AVERY / PHOTOGRAPHIC RESOURCES

The Hollenberg Pony Express Station, constructed in 1857 on the Oregon-California Trail, near Hanover, Washington County
JOHN AVERY / PHOTOGRAPHIC RESOURCES

Pony Express statue in Marysville, Marshall County   BILL & JAN MOELLER

Kansas Museum of History in Topeka   BOB BARRETT

Cedar Crest Governor's Mansion, built in 1928, in Topeka   NORMA WATTS

The State Capitol, started in 1866 and completed in 1903, beyond the Fountain of Justice in Topeka
JOHN AVERY/ /PHOTOGRAPHIC RESOURCES

" *Kansans made the government themselves for their own purposes. It is the sum of the energy, the good judgment, the resourcefulness of the individuals who originally created it, and who periodically renew it. The government is the individual writ large; in it every Kansan sees himself drawn to larger scale.* "

Carl L. Becker,
"Kansas"

Loading a cannon with help from uniformed volunteers at Fort Scott National Historic Site   STEVE HARPER

" *The belief that Kansas was
founded for a cause distinguishes
it, in the eyes of its inhabitants,
as pre-eminently the home of
freedom.* "

Carl L. Becker,
"Kansas"

Celebrating the dedication of Eisenhower State Park near Junction City
MIKE BLAIR

Part of the annual Fourth of July fireworks at the State Fairgrounds in Hutchinson   MIKE BLAIR

Vast field of corn, Kansas' second leading crop after wheat, near Great Bend, Barton County   LARRY FLEMING

> *How our friends in the east would pity us if they knew just how we live, yet I dare say there is not one in a hundred who enjoys the half we do....We have pure fresh air, fine spirits and feel that to live in a land like this is a joy.*

Sara T. Robinson
Kansas—Its Interior and Exterior Life (1856)

65

Harvesting corn in Stafford County   MIKE BLAIR

Hot-air balloons drifting peacefully over wheat fields near Newton LARRY FLEMING

Colorful catamarans ready to launch on Perry Lake northeast of Topeka   DANIEL DANCER

Fishing for bluegills at the Dillon Nature Center in Hutchinson
MIKE BLAIR

> " 'All you have to do is to knock the heels together three times and command the shoes to carry you wherever you wish to go.'
>
> 'If that is so,' said the child joyfully, 'I will ask them to carry me back to Kansas at once.' "
>
> **Frank L. Baum,**
> The Wizard of Oz

Keyhole Arch at Monument Rocks National Landmark, Gove County   STEVE MULLIGAN

> **"** *I like Kansas—that is, natural Kansas—better than I had expected to.* **"**

Horace Greeley,
An Overland Journey

Peaceful morning along the Ninnescah River near Kingman   MIKE BLAIR

Whitetail buck in north-central Kansas   FRANK OBERLE

Sunset at John Redmond Reservoir near Burlington, Coffey County   DANIEL DANCER

Stones left by Ice Age glaciers on a prairie hilltop in Wabaunsee County   STEVE MULLIGAN

" This is a country where even to look at the landscape is to accept a dare....It can be exhilarating to try to feel significant in such an enormous place. "

Peg Wherry,
''Straight Roads''

Tallgrass prairie in the Flint Hills, near Alma   DAVID MUENCH

Perfect day for fishing a prairie pond in the Flint Hills   STEVE HARPER

66 Kansans young and old love their state. When she was seven, our daughter Dorothy visited her aunt on a Missouri farm and longed for home before the time appointed to return. As our car crossed the state line and entered Kansas, she sighed, 'The air is better already.' 99

Zula Bennington Greene,
Kansas in Color

Playing as a thunderstorm gathers momentum in Wichita   JOEL SARTORE

Storm clouds glowing at sunset in Johnson County   BOB BARRETT

An autumn sky over Reno County   STEVE HARPER

" *Yes. The sky is better than television sometimes. I remember one incredible sunset that I watched all the way from Coldwater one winter evening. . . .There were four of us in the car. . .and the conversation trailed off as the sky changed. We were all watching it, but no one wanted to be the first goop to say so. Finally Ed ventured an understatement: 'Nice sunset, isn't it?' Oh yes.* "

Peg Wherry,
"Straight Roads"

Kansas sunset, Sedgwick County   LARRY FLEMING

Cottonwoods, the state trees, at the Big Grove, Scott County State Park STEVE MULLIGAN

" *The cottonwood is not a sturdy or long-lived tree, like the oak. Its wood is not valued, like the walnut's. It does not even make good firewood. But it has an airy grace that pays its way.* *"*

Zula Bennington Greene,
"The Cottonwood"

Fox squirrel in Coffeyville MIKE LOGAN

Cottonwoods, the "pioneer tree of Kansas," and limestone fenceposts cut by pioneers, in Clark County   DANIEL DANCER

Cattle grazing in the Chautauqua Hills near Sedan   STEVE HARPER

"Kansans do not regard themselves as mere westerners, like Iowans or Nebraskans. Having passed through a superior heat, they are westerners seven times refined."

Carl L. Becker,
"Kansas"

Chase County cowhands moving cattle during an annual fall roundup   STEVE HARPER

Longhorns in southwest Kansas   FRANK OBERLE

Bullrider in motion at the Strong City Rodeo   NATHAN HAM

Flag-bearers at the Pretty Prairie Rodeo   JOEL SARTORE

Barndance at the Land Institute's annual Prairie Festival, Salina   GEORGE OLSON

Hoping for a lucky number at the Cheyenne County Fair   STEVE HARPER

A great blue heron surveying a sunset at Harvey County East Lake   STEVE HARPER

Storm clouds gathering above Canada geese
on Wyandotte County Lake   BOB BARRETT

Worth boasting about: a spectacular lightning display in Kingman County   MIKE BLAIR

" *Kansas brags on its thunder and lightning, and the boast is well founded.* "

Horace Greeley,
''An Overland Journey''

Wind-carved and water-eroded badlands along the Smoky Hill River in Gove County BOB GRESS

Poison ivy climbing a sandstone wall in Douglas County STEVE MULLIGAN

❝ *This is a far country, high and pale and abstract. Its landscapes are predominantly skyscapes of which, earth or sky, the slightest detail assumes by its very rarity a large significance.* **❞**

Kenneth S. Davis,
"Portrait of a Changing Kansas"

> **"** *I guess if you've never seen or experienced open land such as we have here, it would be difficult to accept. It's just peaceful. Gets you away from the strains of our normal life. You have to adjust to the quietness out here. And, really, loneliness and isolation at times. If you learn to live with yourself, you're going to be all right.* **"**

Elizabeth Rogler,
Chase County rancher,
quoted in Kansas People

Blacktail prairie dog pups near Sterling, Rice County
MIKE BLAIR

High-plains prairie dominated by yucca and sagebrush near Scott City   MIKE BLAIR

Winter in the Arikaree Breaks in Cheyenne County   STEVE MULLIGAN

"The special quality of fine prairie weather isn't necessarily one of intrinsic merit, but of contrast with what has gone just before."

John Madson,
Where the Sky Began

Bluejay waiting out a snowstorm   GERALD J. WIENS

Arikaree River in the extreme northwestern corner of Kansas, Cheyenne County STEVE MULLIGAN

Walking sticks spanning stalks of prairie grass   JOEL SARTORE

Prairie chicken strutting in a mating display, Crawford County   FRANK OBERLE

A pheasant hunter looking for birds in waist-deep milo, near Penalosa, Kingman County   STEVE HARPER

Ring-necked pheasant, Kansas' most popular game species   BOB GRESS

> *" The prairies do not startle you with sudden vivid beauty. . . .They do not dazzle you or exhaust you with excitement. There are no dramatic tricks. They are a quality rather than a quantity.*
>
> *[The prairie] is not the gorgeous woman you dreamed should some day be yours, but she is mystery and tenderness and strength and rapture, and suddenly you know that this is what you wanted all of your life. "*

Zula Bennington Greene,
"Prairie"

96

Western meadowlark, Kansas' state bird, in full song
FRANK OBERLE

Bison, Kansas' state animal, cresting a ridge on the Konza Prairie   FRANK OBERLE

Burning the prairie in the Flint Hills, west of Matfield Green   STEVE HARPER

" *[Kansas is] a state like nothing so much as some scriptural kingdom—a land of floods, droughts, cyclones, and enormous crops, of prophets and plagues.* "

Julian Street,
Abroad at Home

Summer sunrise in Dickinson County   STEVE HARPER

A rotary plow on bromegrass in northern Morris County   STEVE HARPER

Crop-dusting wheat with a Cessna Husky near Smith Center, geographical center of the United States JOEL SARTORE

“ *It is precisely because Kansans are such thoroughgoing individualists, so resourceful, so profoundly confident in their own judgments, so emancipated from the past, so accustomed to devising expedients for every new difficulty, that they are unimpressed by the record of the world's failures. They have always thrived on the impossible. . . .* ”

Carl L. Becker,
"Kansas"

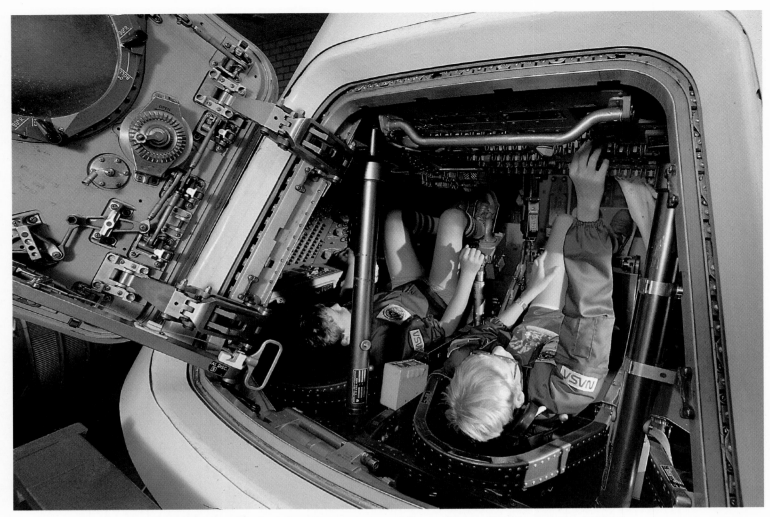

Hands-on experience at the Cosmosphere and Space Center, Hutchinson   BOB BARRETT

" *The Kansas spirit is the American spirit double distilled. It is a new grafted product of American individualism, American idealism, American intolerance. Kansas is America in microcosm....* "

Carl L. Becker,
"Kansas"

Rocket engine on display at the Cosmosphere and Space Center
BOB BARRETT

A towering thunderstorm meets a crescent moon over the Flint Hills near Bazaar   JOEL SARTORE

Dawn inspection of a B-1 bomber at McConnell Air Force Base, Wichita   JOEL SARTORE

Fort Larned, key military post along the Santa Fe Trail, now a National Historic Site BILL & JAN MOELLER

Grant Hall at Fort Leavenworth
JOHN AVERY / PHOTOGRAPHIC RESOURCES

Cavalry Museum at Fort Riley BOB BARRETT

The Z-Bar Ranch House, built in 1881, north of Strong City   STEVE HARPER

Geese migrating across the Kansas sky near the Quivira National Wildlife Refuge, Stafford County   JOEL SARTORE

"*God made the world, and rested. And then, to make creation doubly-sweet, he made the state of Kansas.*"

John Clum Bradshaw

Blossoms of butterfly milkweed gracing the graceful Flint Hills, south of Strong City   FRANK OBERLE

Fragrant water lilies in a pond near Hutchinson   MIKE BLAIR

Snowy egrets searching for food at Cheyenne Bottoms   STEVE HARPER

Red-headed duck at Cheyenne Bottoms   FRANK OBERLE

As colorful as its name implies, an ornate box turtle, the Kansas state reptile   GERALD J. WIENS

Grasshopper on bur oak leaves   STEVE HARPER

“ *The beauty of the heartland can be striking and elusive. With its own brand of magic, it has romanticism spelled out in effort. A spirit that must be explored.... If you dig deep enough and peel enough away, you can reach a level of truth that is authentic and the pure essence of the past.* ”

Lyle Alan White,
The Pioneer Spirit, A Prairie Portrait

Pillsbury Crossing on Deep Creek along the Santa Fe Trail, Wabaunsee County STEVE MULLIGAN

> *When civilization . . . shall have transformed this glorious country from what it now is to the brilliant destiny awaiting it, the sun in all his course will visit no land more truly lovely and desirable than this . . . .*

Cyrus Kurtz Holliday,
"Letters of Cyrus Kurtz Holliday, 1854-1859"

Sand Hill plums to be made into jelly   STEVE HARPER

113

Red, ripe, and ready for picking: Sand Hill plums near Coats, Barber County STEVE HARPER

Historical buildings at the Prairie Museum of Art and History, Colby   JOHN AVERY / PHOTOGRAPHIC RESOURCES

Young participants in the Indian Peace Treaty Pageant, Medicine Lodge   LARRY FLEMING

Abandoned homestead and wildflowers in Dickinson County   DANIEL DANCER

Prairie shooting stars   FRANK OBERLE

❝ *It was a dream that brought us here,"* said a pioneer. *"And it's a dream we gotta pass on.* **❞**

The Pioneer Spirit, A Prairie Portrait

White ash in autumn colors, Cherokee County   STEVE MULLIGAN

"" Kansas, as now accepted, written and spoken, is one of the most beautiful Indian words adapted to use in the English tongue. As a name for a state it is unequalled. ""

William E. Connelley,
A Standard History of Kansas and Kansans

Mourning dove in sumac tree, Sedgwick County
BOB GRESS

Virginia creeper on a cottonwood tree, Barber County   STEVE MULLIGAN

they made it possible

Kansas is a colorful and beautiful state—if one knows where and when to look. Fortunately, Kansas is blessed with many photographers who not only know where to look, they know how to capture the best of what they see on film. For *Kansas on My Mind,* these photographers submitted their finest images, and the result shows in this stunning collection of photos. What does not show is the work it took to get these images— the early mornings to capture sunrise, the long drives through lonely landscapes, the endless hours of waiting for the perfect light, the hundreds of shots that didn't turn out quite right, and the high level of technical skills that were acquired through years of experience and study.

To all the photographers who contributed to *Kansas on My Mind,* we say thanks. We appreciate their art and their hard work.

Michael S. Sample and Bill Schneider
Publishers, Falcon Press

Photographers in *Kansas on My Mind*

Neal Allen
John Avery/
    Photographic Resources
Bob Barrett
Mike Blair
Jon Blumb
Daniel Dancer
Larry Fleming
Bob Gress
Nathan Ham
Steve Harper
Mike Logan
Bill & Jan Moeller
David Muench
Steve Mulligan
Frank Oberle
George Olson
Anthony Reed
Joel Sartore
Tom Till
Norma Watts
Gerald J. Wiens

Published in cooperation with *The Wichita Eagle*

Copyright © 1993 by Falcon Press Publishing Co., Inc. Helena and Billings, Montana

Design, typesetting, and other prepress work by Falcon Press, Helena, Montana. Printed in Korea.

Library of Congress Number: 93-071196

ISBN 1-56044-206-9

For extra copies of this book
Please check with your local bookstore, or contact Book Kansas! at 1-800-825-6397 ext. 6620, P.O. Box 820, Wichita, KS 67201-0820.

You also may write Falcon Press, P.O. Box 1718, Helena, MT 59624 or call toll-free 1-800-582-2665.

AMERICA
on my mind
series

acknowledgments

The publisher gratefully acknowledges the following sources:

Page 16, 89 from "Portrait of a Changing Kansas" by Kenneth S. Davis in *What Kansas Means to Me.* Copyright © 1991 by University Press of Kansas, Lawrence, Kansas. Originally published in the *Kansas Historical Quarterly,* Spring 1976.

Page 19 from *PrairyErth* by William Least Heat-Moon. Copyright © 1991 by William Least Heat-Moon; Houghton Mifflin Company, Boston.

Page 20 from "Touching the Sky," an original essay by Denise Low in *What Kansas Means to Me.* Copyright © 1991 by University Press of Kansas, Lawrence, Kansas.

Page 32 from "The Great Kansas Passage" by William Least Heat-Moon in *What Kansas Means to Me.* Copyright © 1991 by the University Press of Kansas, Lawrence, Kansas. Originally published in *The Four Seasons of Kansas.* Copyright © 1988 by University Press of Kansas, Lawrence, Kansas.

Page 37 from "Blue Grass" by John James Ingalls in *A Collection of the Writings of John James Ingalls.* Copyright © 1902 by Hudson-Kimberly Publishing Company, Kansas City, Missouri.

Page 38 from "A Level Land" by William Inge in *What Kansas Means to Me.* Copyright © 1991 by University Press of Kansas, Lawrence, Kansas. Originally published as the introduction to *The Plains States: Iowa, Kansas, Minnesota, Missouri, Nebraska, North Dakota, South Dakota* by Evan Jones and the editors of Time-Life Books, New York. Copyright © 1968.

Page 41, 61, 62, 84, 101, 102 from "Kansas" by Carl L. Becker in *What Kansas Means to Me.* Copyright © 1991 by University Press of Kansas, Lawrence, Kansas. Originally published in *Essays in American History Dedicated to Frederick Jackson Turner.* Copyright © 1910 by Henry Holt & Company, New York.

Page 45, 46, 90 from *Kansas People* by Larry Hatteberg. Copyright © 1991 by Jular Publishing, Wichita, Kansas.

Page 49 from *Natural Kansas* edited by Joseph Collins. Copyright © 1985 by University Press of Kansas, Lawrence, Kansas.

Page 65 from *Kansas-Its Interior and Exterior Life* by Sara T. Robinson in *Kansas in Color* edited by Andrea Glenn. Copyright © 1982 by the University Press of Kansas, Lawrence, Kansas. Originally published in 1856 by Crosby, Nichols & Company, Boston.

Page 67 from *The Wizard of Oz* by Frank L. Baum. Copyright © 1982 by Henry Holt & Co., New York, NY.

Page 69, 83 from *An Overland Journey* by Horace Greeley in *PrairyErth* by William Least Heat-Moon. Copyright © 1991 by William Least Heat-Moon. Houghton Mifflin Company, Boston. Originally published by C.M. Saxton, Barker & Co. Copyright © 1860.

Page 72, 77 from "Straight Roads" by Peg Wherry in *What Kansas Means to Me.* Copyright © 1991 by University Press of Kansas, Lawrence, Kansas. Originally published in *North American Review,* Vol. 267, No. 2, June 1982.

Page 74 from the introduction to "Kansas in Color" by Zula Bennington Greene. Copyright © 1982 by University Press of Kansas, Lawrence, Kansas.

Page 80 from "The Cottonwood" by Zula Bennington Greene in *What Kansas Means to Me.* Copyright © 1991 by University Press of Kansas, Lawrence, Kansas. Originally published in the *Topeka Capital.* Reprinted in *Kansas Magazine,* 1945.

Page 92 from *Where the Sky Began* by John Madson. Copyright © 1982 by Houghton Mifflin Company, Boston.

Page 96 from "Prairie" by Zula Bennington Greene in *What Kansas Means to Me.* Copyright © 1991 by University Press of Kansas, Lawrence, Kansas. Originally published in the *Topeka Capital.* Reprinted in *Kansas Magazine,* 1945.

Page 98 from *Abroad At Home* by Julian Street in *PrairyErth* by William Least-Heat Moon. Copyright © 1991 by William Least-Heat Moon. Houghton Mifflin Company, Boston. Originally published by The Century Co. Copyright © 1914.

Page 112 from "Letters of Cyrus Kurtz Holliday, 1854-1859" by Karl A. Menninger in *What Kansas Means to Me.* Copyright © 1991 by University Press of Kansas, Lawrence, Kansas. Originally published in *Kansas Magazine,* 1939.

Page 110, 115 from *The Pioneer Spirit, A Prairie Portrait* by Lyle Alan White. Copyright © 1986 by Lyle Alan White. Walter Publications/The Lowell Press, Kansas City.

Page 116 from *A Standard History of Kansas and Kansans* by William E. Connelley in *PrairyErth* by William Least-Heat Moon. Copyright © 1991 by William Least-Heat Moon. Houghton Mifflin Company, Boston. Originally published by Lewis Publishing Company. Copyright © 1918-1919.

About Steve Harper

Steve Harper is forty-eight years old, a native of Newton in Harvey County, and is a third generation Kansan. His family came to Kansas by covered wagon in the early 1880s and settled on West Emma Creek west of Newton. Harper, his wife Charlotte, and their three daughters, are the fourth generation to live in the family homeplace at Newton.

For the past four years, Harper has been the outdoor writer for *The Wichita Eagle.* Prior to that he was Director of Photography at *The Eagle* for nine-and-one-half years. He came to the newspaper in 1979 after teaching photojournalism and graphic design at Wichita State University for six-and-one-half years. In 1971 Harper received his undergraduate degree in Motion Pictures from Brooks Institute of Photography and Fine Arts at Santa Barbara, California.

In the summers of 1985, 1988, and 1989 Harper wrote a series of weekly columns for *The Eagle* on Kansas Day Trips. Those columns culminated in Harper's book, *83,000 Square Miles, No Lines, No Waiting - Kansas Day Trips.* The book has sold more than 10,000 copies and continues to be the newspaper's best seller.

Harper has won more than fifteen national and regional awards in photojournalism, and has been involved in ten fine arts photography exhibitions including three one-man shows. In 1989 he co-produced a hardbound book, *Artists: A Kansas Collection,* for the Artists Registry of Kansas.

Day's end for a harvest crew near Winfield   JOEL SARTORE

❝ *I've never met a Kansan anywhere whose heart wasn't buried in Kansas.* ❞

Kenneth S. Davis,
quoting a friend